STUDENT EXAMINATION SHEET

PIANO (TO BE HANDED TO EXAMINER AT TIME OF EXAMINATION)

TEACHER: Mrs Switzer

DATE GIVEN TO STUDENT: ____

NAME OF STUDENT: Lauren Dykstra

ADDRESS: ____

AGE: 15

GRADE: 5

SELECTIONS
- A: Jazz Hymn — p.10
- B: It Takes Two — p.14
- C: Breakfast Time — p.29

TECHNICAL WORK – All work to be played BY MEMORY, except studies. (Teacher – State whether hands together or separate in accordance with syllabus).

Chromatic Scale Starting on A H.T. 1oct.

SCALES —
 MAJOR: B+, F+ H.T. 2octs ⟩ Staccato
 MINOR: B-, F- Harmonic & Melodic H.T. 2oct. / H.S. 2octs

TRIADS —
 MAJOR: B+, F+ ⟩ H.T. 2octs
 MINOR: B-, F- / Solid & Broken   w/ V-I cadence

CHORDS —
 MAJOR: ____
 MINOR: ____
 DOMINANT 7TH: B+, F+, B-, F- ⟩ H.S. 1oct
 DIMINISHED 7TH: B-, F- / Solid & Broken

ARPEGGIOS —
 MAJOR: B+, F+ ⟩ H.S.
 MINOR: B-, F- / 2octs
 DOMINANT 7TH: ____
 DIMINISHED 7TH: ____

Formula Patterns: Eb+, G- Harmonic H.T. 2octs.

STUDIES —
 1. Allegro — p.79
 2. Fishpond — p.80

EAR TRAINING — Intervals: +2, +3, -3, P4, P5, +6, -6, P8
 Below: +3, P4, P5, P8

PARENT'S SIGNATURE: ____

american popular piano 5
REPERTOIRE

Compositions by
Christopher Norton

Additional Compositions and Arrangements
Dr. Scott McBride Smith

Editor
Dr. Scott McBride Smith

Associate Editor
Clarke MacIntosh

Stratford, Ontario, Canada

A Note about this Book

Pop music styles can be grouped into three broad categories:

- **lyrical** — pieces with a beautiful singing quality and rich harmonies; usually played at a slow tempo;
- **rhythmic** — more up-tempo pieces, with energetic, catchy rhythms; these often have a driving left hand part;
- **ensemble** — works meant to be played with other musicians, or with backing tracks (or both!); this type of piece requires careful listening and shared energy.

American Popular Piano has been deliberately designed to develop skills in all three areas.

You can integrate the cool, motivating pieces in **American Popular Piano** into your piano studies in several ways.

- pick a piece you like and learn it; when you're done, pick another!
- choose a piece from each category to develop a complete range of skills in your playing;
- polish a particular favorite for your local festival or competition. Works from **American Popular Piano** are featured on the lists of required pieces for many festivals and competitions;
- use the pieces as optional contemporary selections in music examinations;
- Or...just have fun!

Going hand-in-hand with the repertoire in **American Popular Piano** are the innovative **Etudes Albums** and **Skills Books**, designed to enhance each student's musical experience by building technical and aural skills.

- **Technical Etudes** in both Classical and Pop Styles are based on musical ideas and technical challenges drawn from the repertoire. Practice these to improve your chops!
- **Improvisation Etudes** offer an exciting new approach to improvisation that guides students effortlessly into spontaneous creativity. Not only does the user-friendly module structure integrate smoothly into traditional lessons, it opens up a whole new understanding of the repertoire being studied.
- **Skills Books** help students develop key supporting skills in sight-reading, ear-training and technique; presented in complementary study modules that are both practical and effective.

Use all of the elements of **American Popular Piano** together to incorporate a comprehensive course of study into your everyday routine. The carefully thought-out pacing makes learning almost effortless. Making music and real progress has never been so much fun!

Library and Archives Canada Cataloguing in Publication

Norton, Christopher, 1953-

American popular piano [music] : repertoire / compositions by Christopher Norton ;
additional compositions and arrangements, Scott McBride Smith ;
editor, Scott McBride Smith ; associate editor, S. Clarke MacIntosh.

To be complete in 11 volumes.
The series is organized in 11 levels, from preparatory to level 10, each including a repertoire album,
an etudes album, a skills book, and an instrumental backings compact disc.

ISBN 1-897379-00-5 (preparatory level).--ISBN 1-897379-01-3 (level 1).--
ISBN 1-897379-02-1 (level 2).--ISBN 1-897379-03-X (level 3).--
ISBN 1-897379-04-8 (level 4).--ISBN 1-897379-05-6 (level 5)

1. Piano music--Teaching pieces. I. Smith, Scott McBride II. MacIntosh, S. Clarke, 1959- III. Title.

LEVEL 5 REPERTOIRE
Table of Contents

A Note about this Book......................................ii

Lyrical
Picnic...2
That Blue Feeling...4
Forgotten Memories 6
In a Glider...7
Waving..8
Jazz Hymn...10
In the Fresh Air...11
Growing Together 12

Rhythmic
It Takes Two 14
A Good Day 15
Locomotive Blues..16
Pixies in the Moonlight 18
Grizzly...20
Tropical Groove...21
The Jogger 22
Taking things in Stride....................................24

Ensemble
A Tender Thought 26
Breakfast Time..28
The Showman 30
Fly Me Away 32
Back on Holiday..36
Floating Away...38
Left Behind 40
Workout..44

Glossary 46

Picnic

Christopher Norton

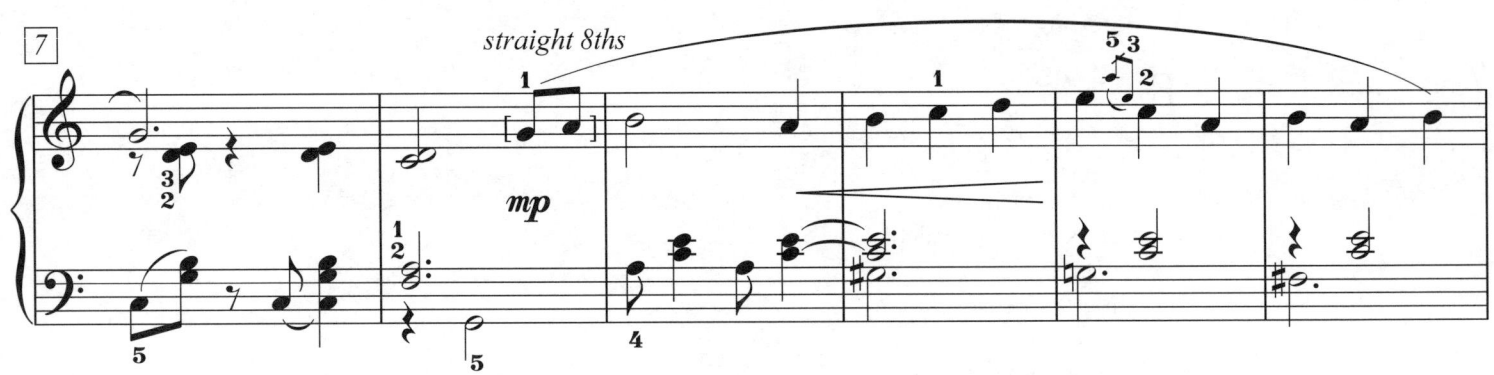
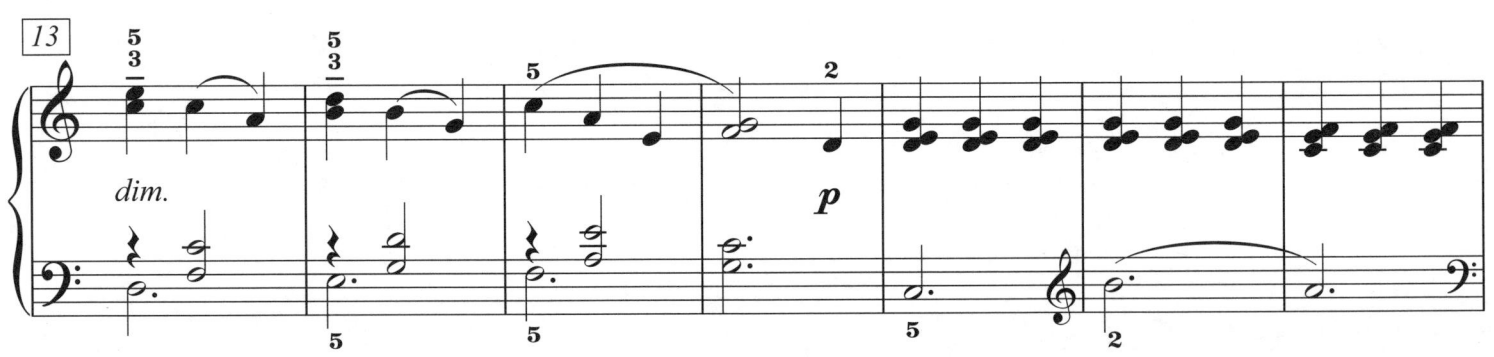
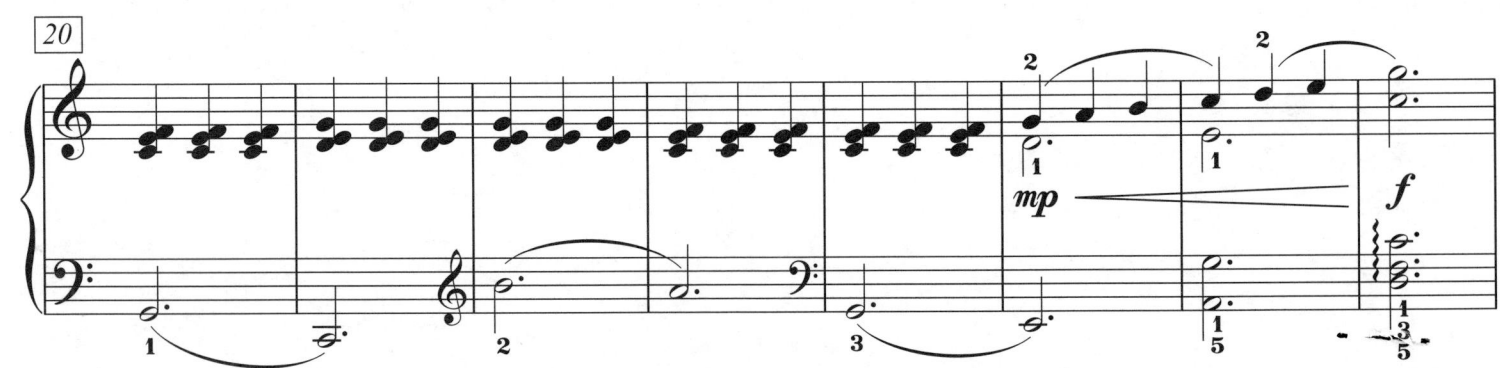

© Novus Via Music Group Inc. 2006. All rights reserved.

Pachelbel's Canon in D

Secondo

Johann Pachelbel

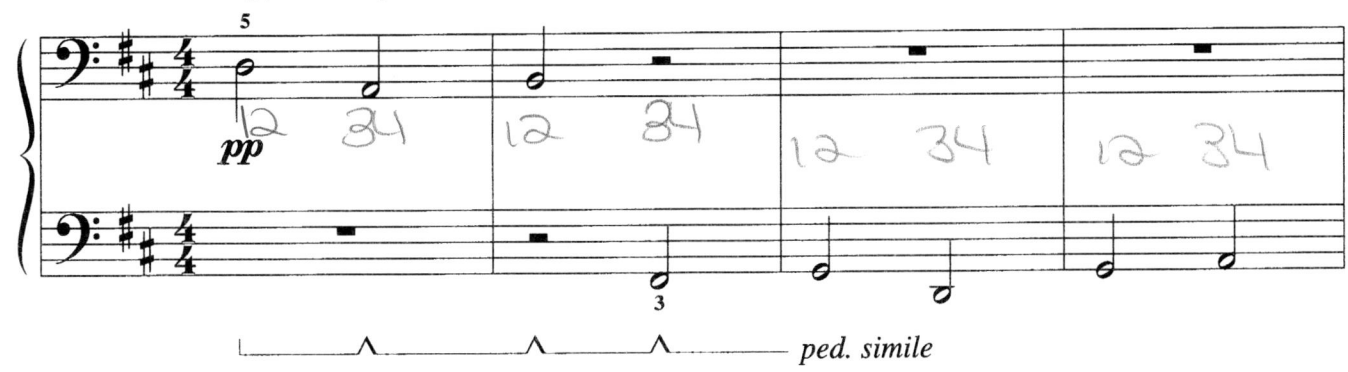

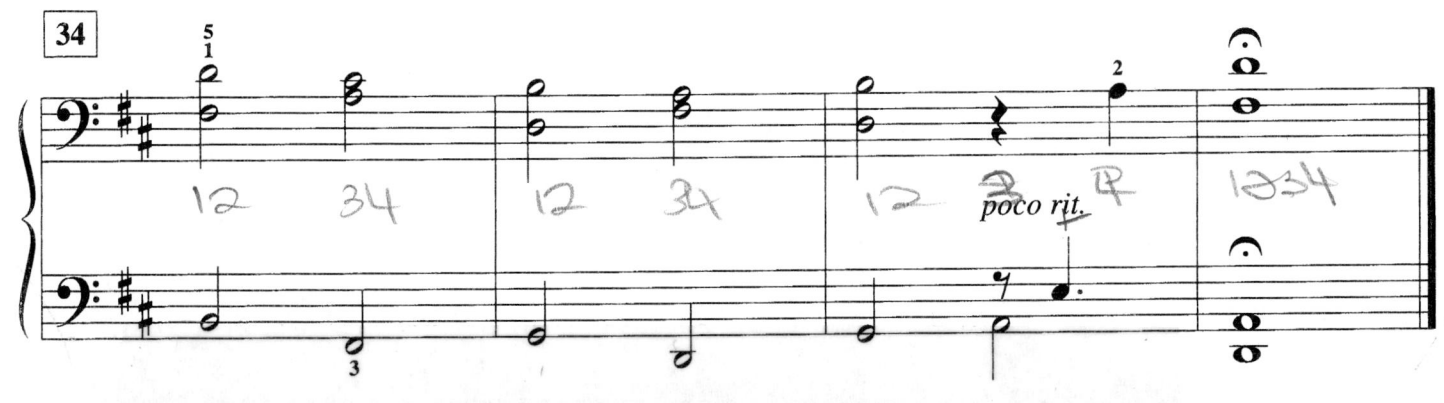

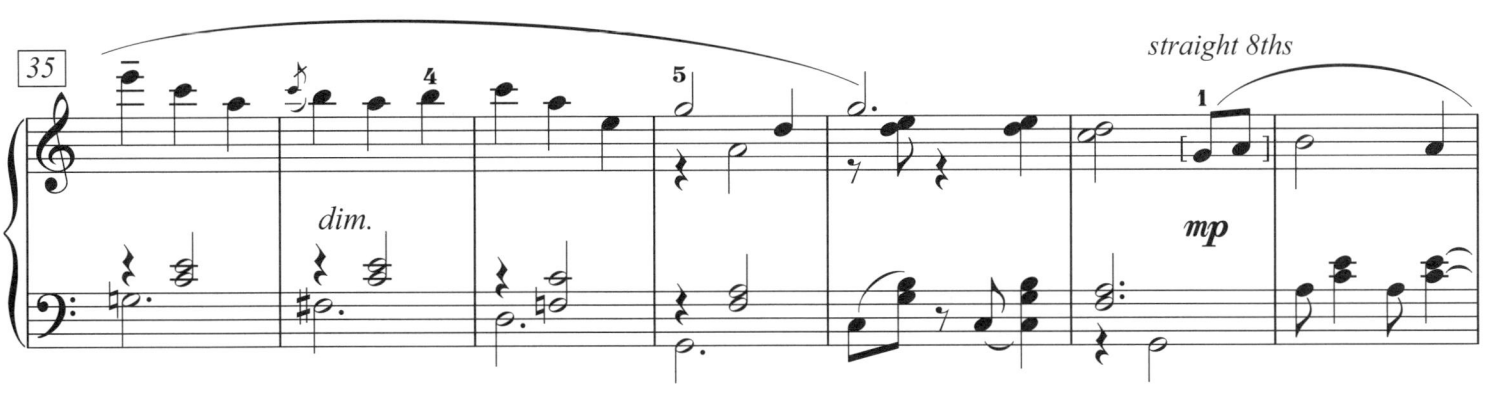

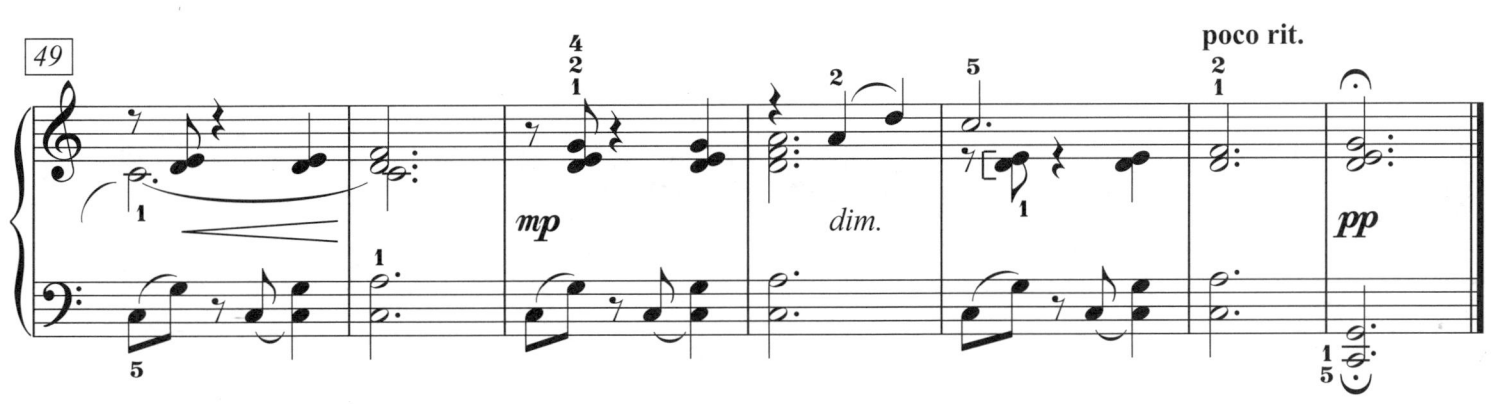

That Blue Feeling

Christopher Norton

Forgotten Memories

Christopher Norton

In A Glider

Christopher Norton

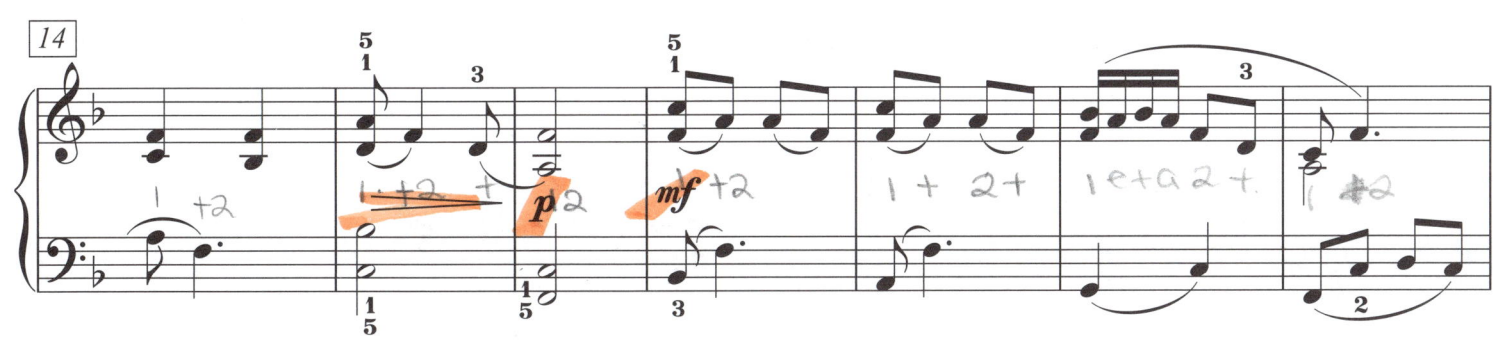
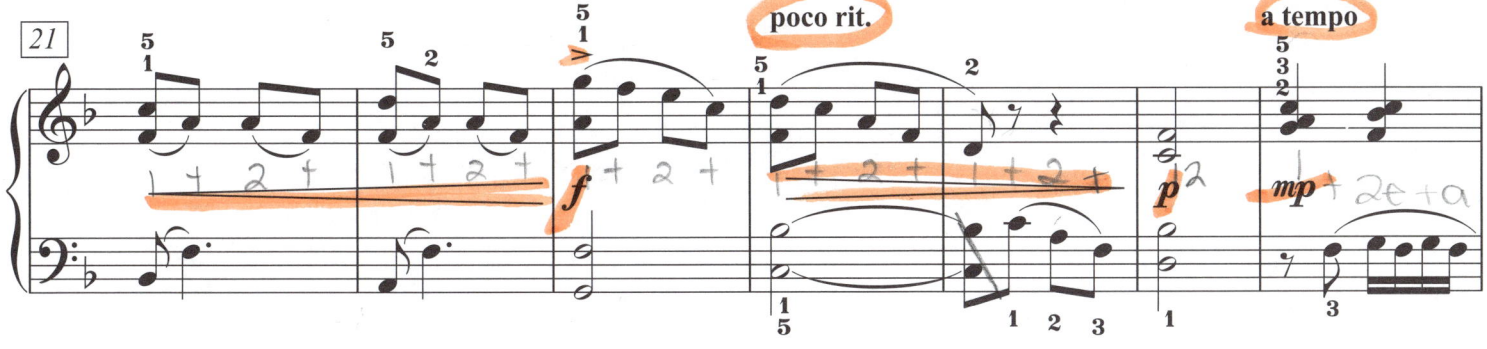

© Novus Via Music Group Inc. 2006. All rights reserved.

Waving

Christopher Norton

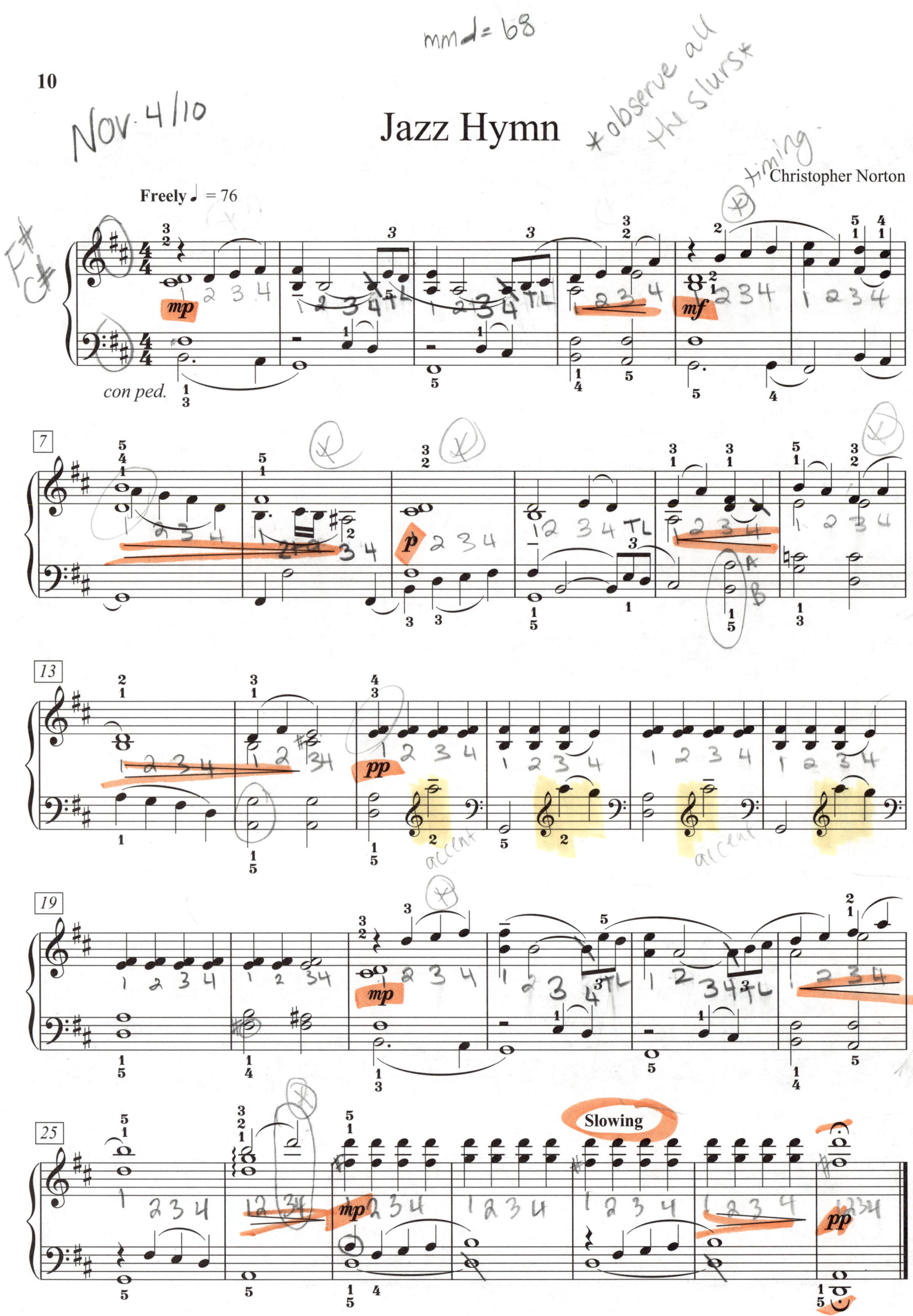

In The Fresh Air

Christopher Norton

Growing Together

Christopher Norton

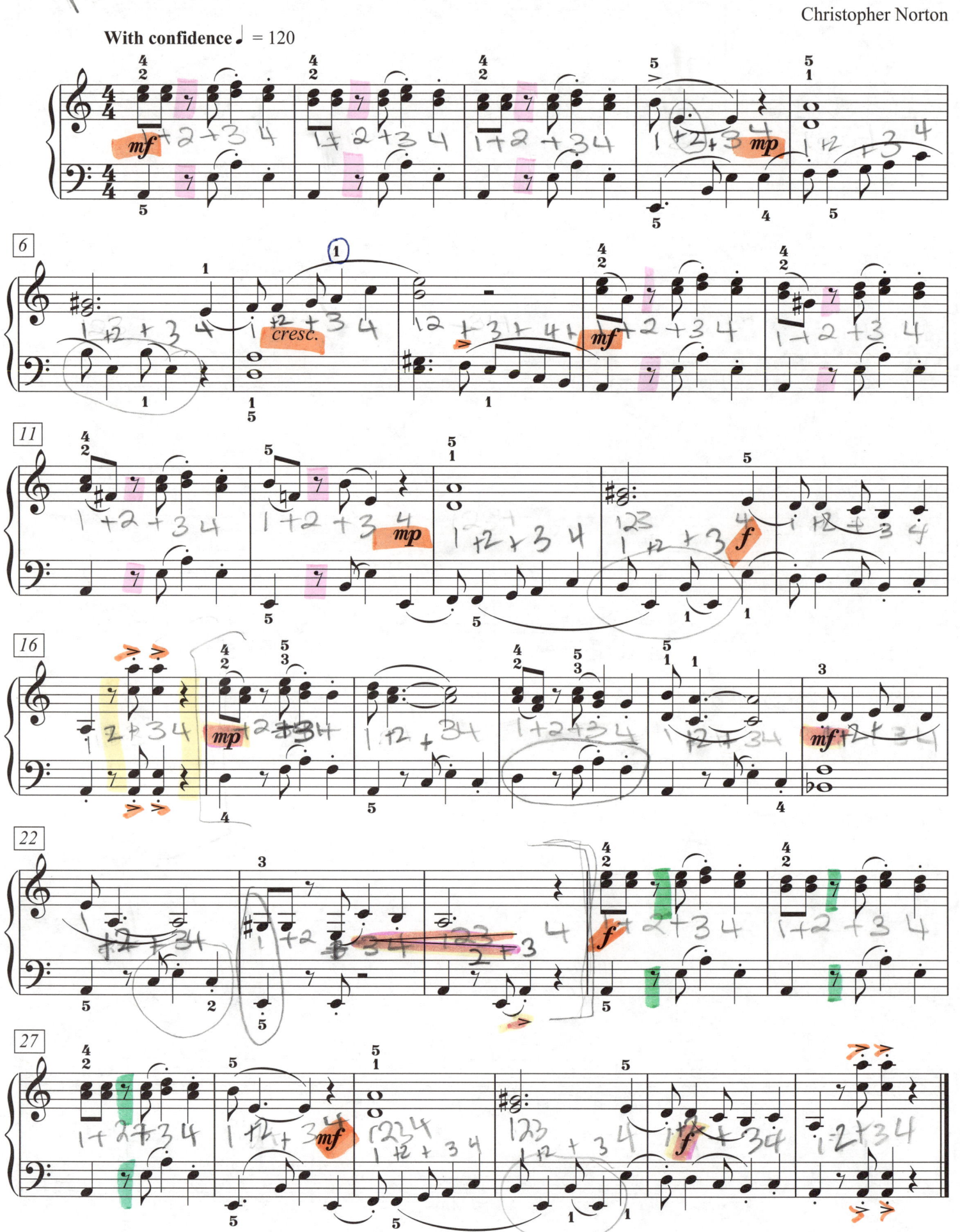

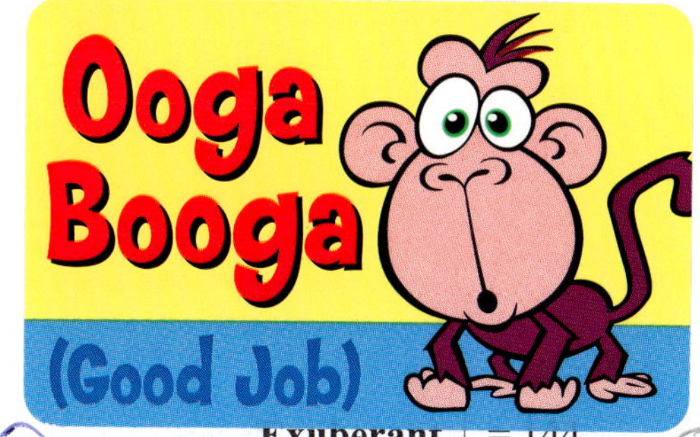

A Good Day

Christopher Norton

Exuberant ♩ = 144
swung 8ths

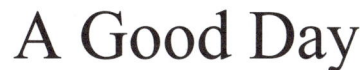

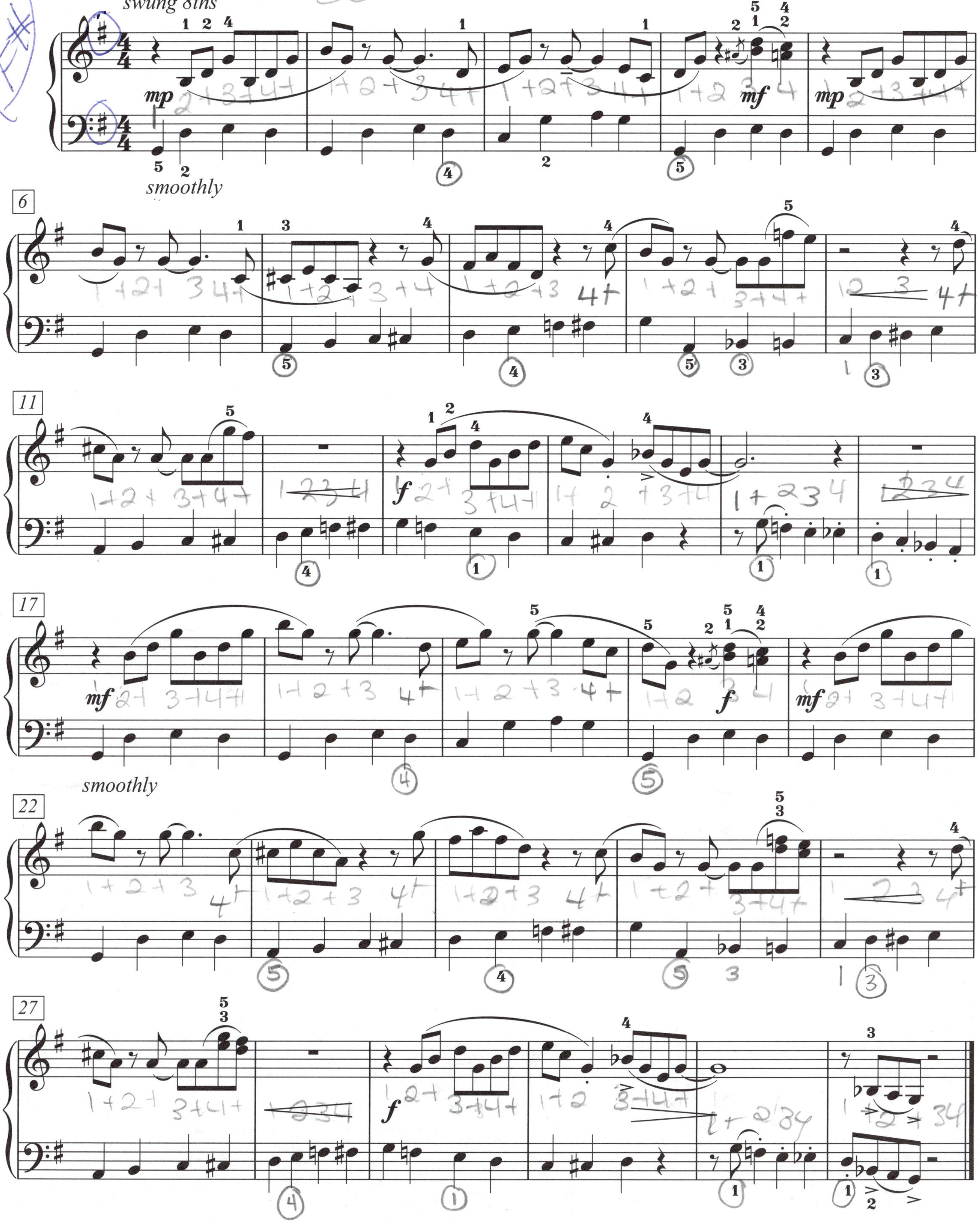

Locomotive Blues

Christopher Norton

© Novus Via Music Group Inc. 2006. All rights reserved.

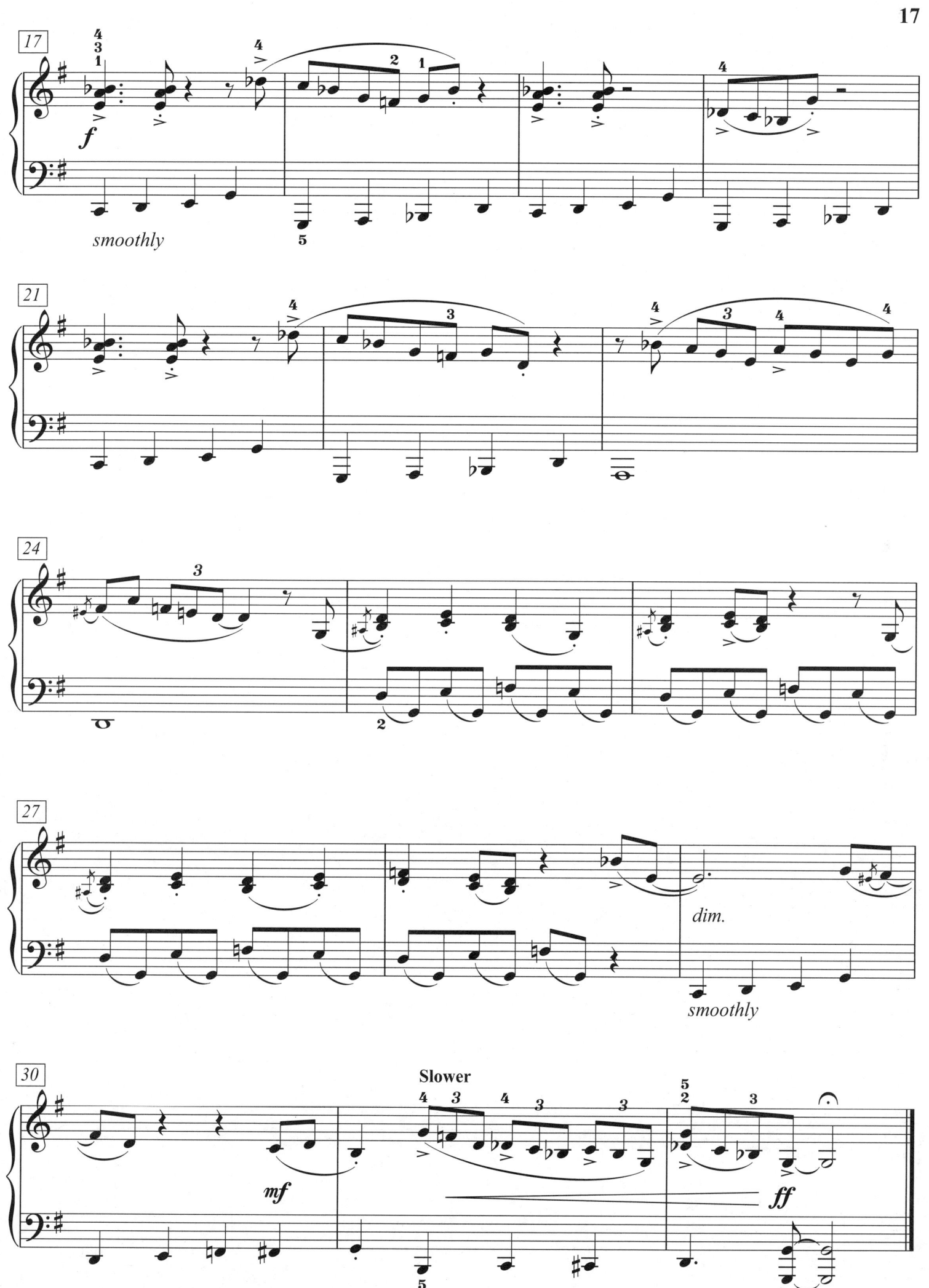

Pixies In The Moonlight

Christopher Norton

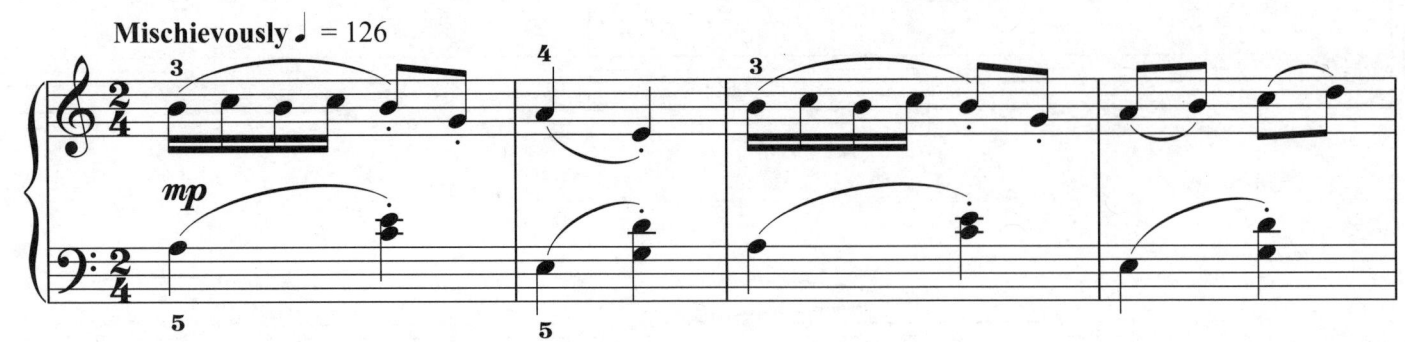
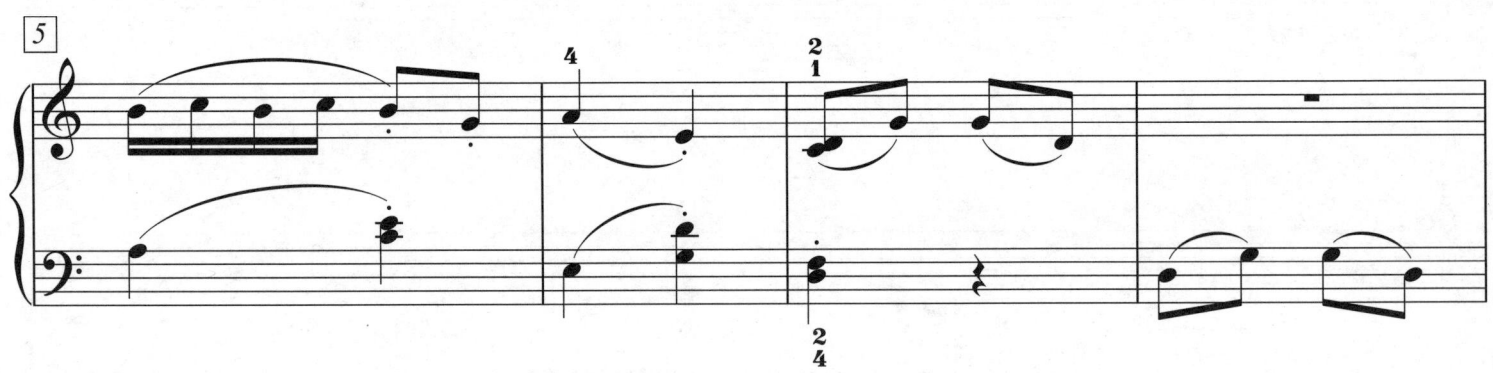

© Novus Via Music Group Inc. 2006. All rights reserved.

Grizzly

Christopher Norton

Tropical Groove

Christopher Norton

D.S. al coda
© Novus Via Music Group Inc. 2006. All rights reserved.

The Jogger

Christopher Norton

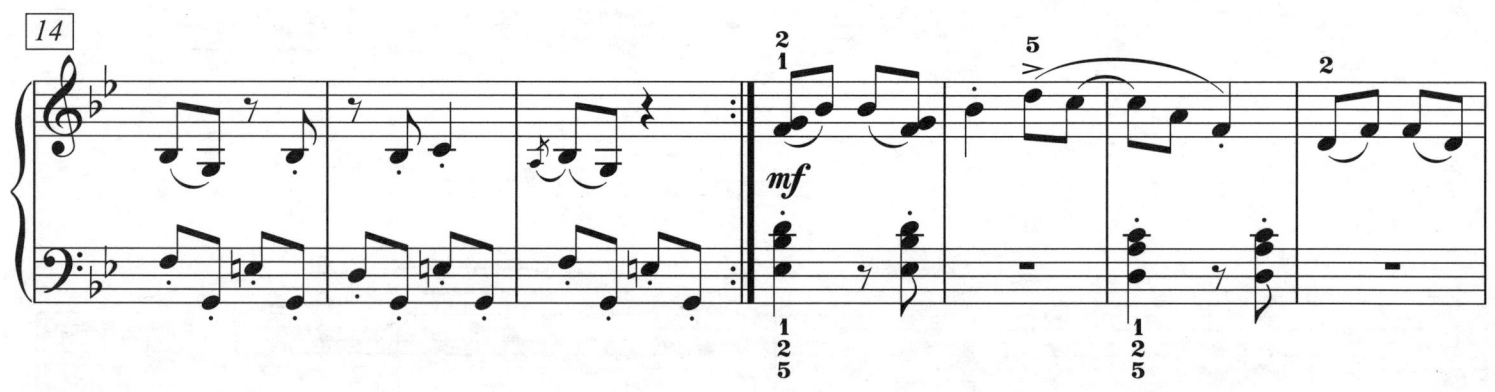

© Novus Via Music Group Inc. 2006. All rights reserved.

24

Taking Things In Stride

Christopher Norton

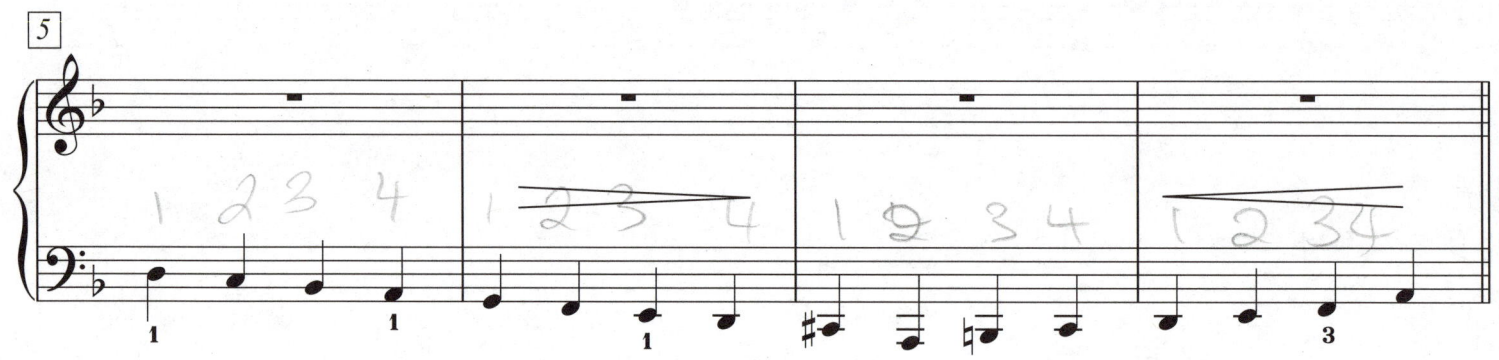
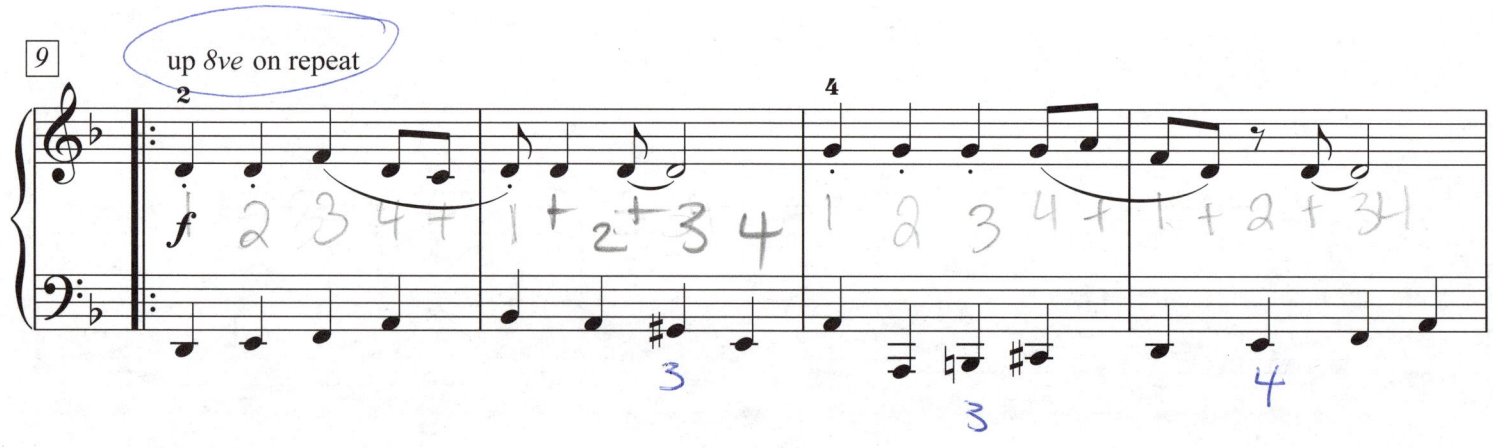
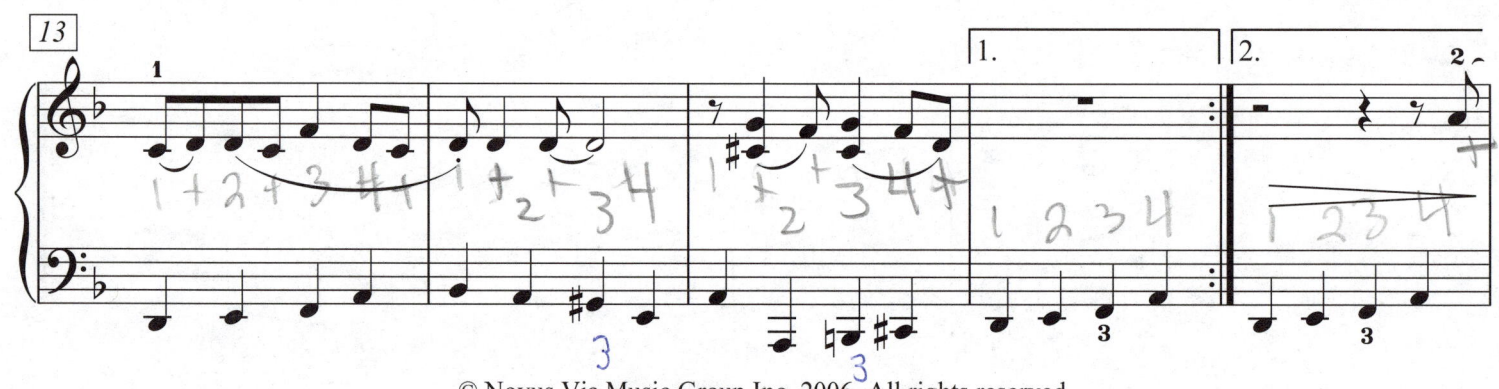

© Novus Via Music Group Inc. 2006. All rights reserved.

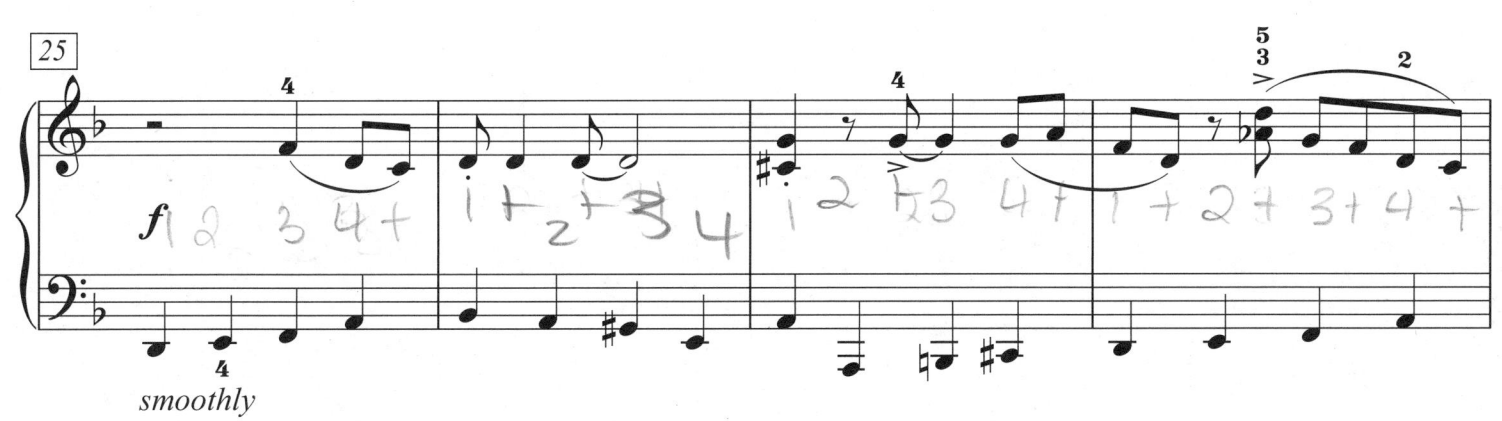

RHYTHM SECTION

A Tender Thought

When played on one piano,
Piano Solo plays as written.

Christopher Norton

© Novus Via Music Group Inc. 2006. All rights reserved.

PIANO SOLO

A Tender Thought

Christopher Norton

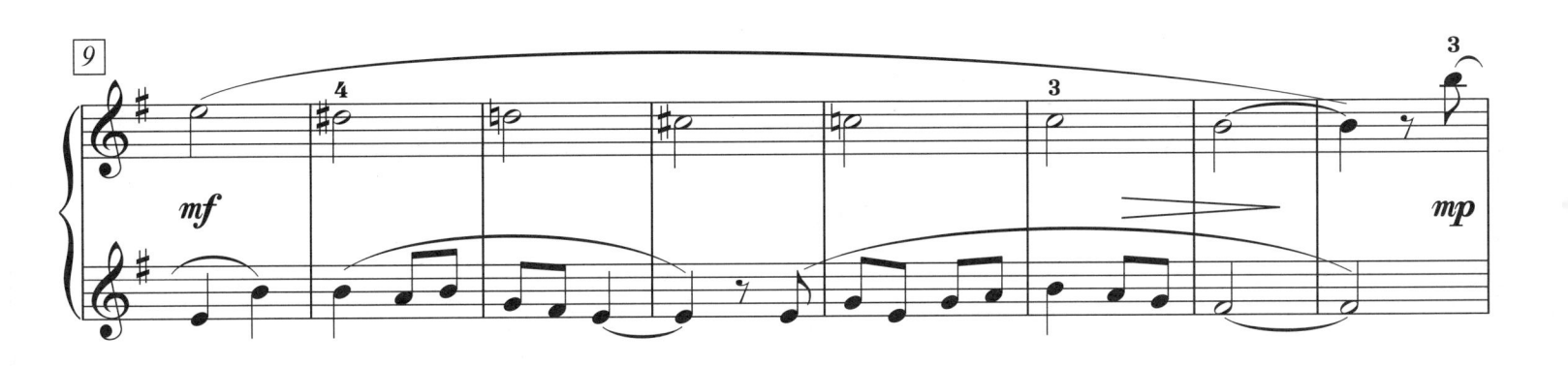

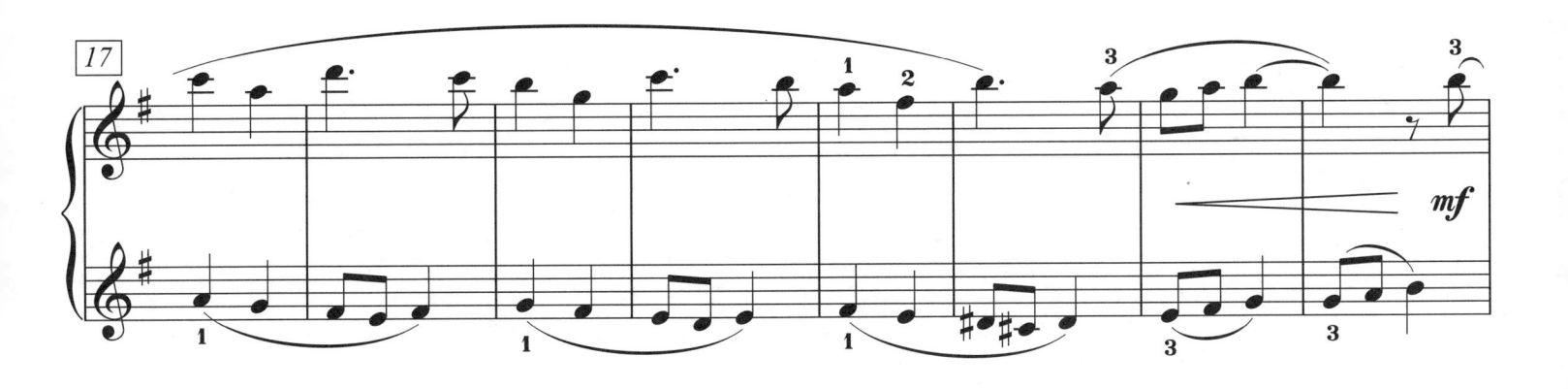

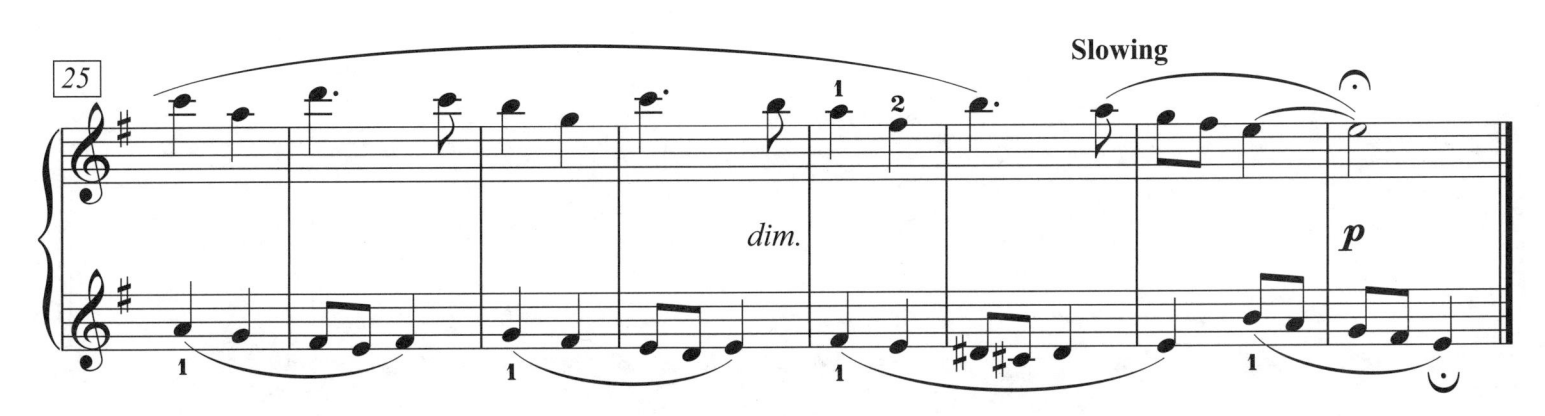

Breakfast Time

RHYTHM SECTION

When played on one piano,
Piano Solo plays one octave higher.

Christopher Norton

Happily ♩ = 138

PIANO SOLO

Breakfast Time

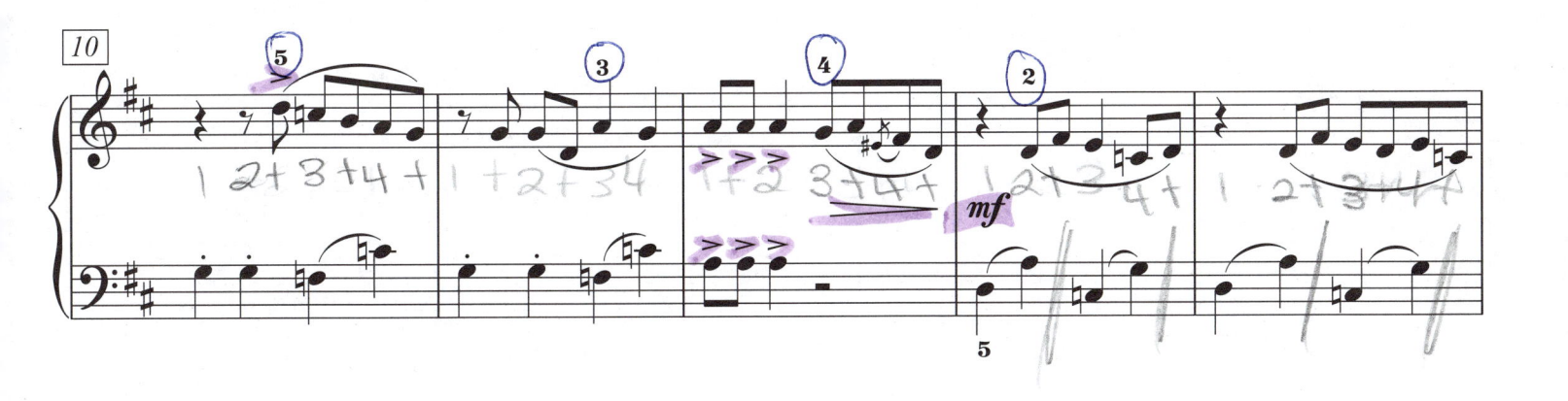

Christopher Norton

© Novus Via Music Group Inc. 2006. All rights reserved.

The Showman

RHYTHM SECTION

When played on one piano,
Piano Solo plays as written.

Christopher Norton

Strutting ♩ = 92

PIANO SOLO

The Showman

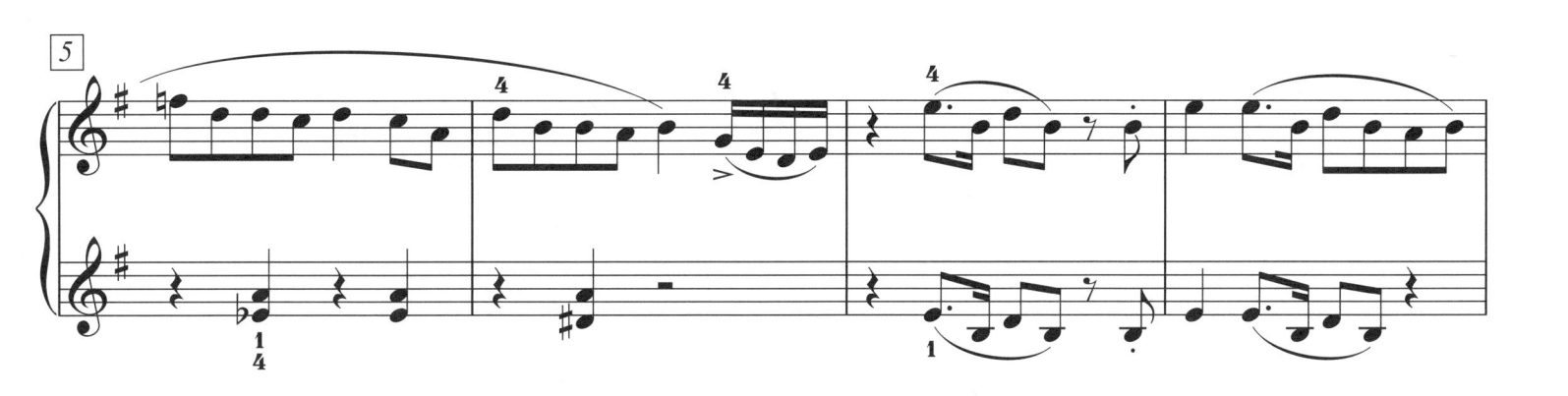

Christopher Norton

Fly Me Away

RHYTHM SECTION

When played on one piano,
Piano Solo plays as written.

Christopher Norton

Confident ♩ = 140

swung 8ths

© Novus Via Music Group Inc. 2006. All rights reserved.

PIANO SOLO

Fly Me Away

Christopher Norton

34 RHYTHM SECTION

PIANO SOLO

RHYTHM SECTION

Back On Holiday

When played on one piano,
Piano Solo plays as written.

Christopher Norton

PIANO SOLO

Back On Holiday

Christopher Norton

With life ♩ = 144

Floating Away

RHYTHM SECTION

When played on one piano,
Piano Solo plays one octave higher.

Christopher Norton

PIANO SOLO

Floating Away

Christopher Norton

D.S. al coda

© Novus Via Music Group Inc. 2006. All rights reserved.

RHYTHM SECTION

Left Behind

Christopher Norton

When played on one piano,
Piano Solo plays one octave higher.

Thoughtfully ♩ = 116

Left Behind

Christopher Norton

42 RHYTHM SECTION

PIANO SOLO

43

44
RHYTHM SECTION

Workout

When played on one piano,
Piano Solo plays one octave higher.

Christopher Norton

With energy ♩ = 108

© Novus Via Music Group Inc. 2006. All rights reserved.

PIANO SOLO

Workout

Christopher Norton

LEVEL 5 REPERTOIRE
Glossary

Backbeat .... Emphasis on beats 2 and 4, in a 4-beat bar. Usually accented by the drums, the backbeat is the most common rhythm in rock music.

Beguine .... A type of Rumba in which the accent is on the second eighth note of the first beat. The style often has strong rhythms supporting flowing, sensuous melodies. Examples include: *Tropical Groove, Begin the Beguine*

Blues .... Musical genre created by African-American musicians, with "blues" notes played against a major-key chord progression often using chords I, IV and V. Examples include: *Heartbreak Hotel*

Blues notes .... A pattern based on a major scale with flat 3rd, 5th, and 7th notes.

Blues shuffle .. A blues chord progression in 12/8, propelled along by the bass or piano left hand. Examples include: *Locomotive Blues, Hound Dog*

Bossa nova .... A Brazilian dance style, with a 2+3+3 eighth note pattern in the right hand over a dotted quarter note, eighth note pattern in the left hand, often with rich, sensuous chords. Examples include: *The Girl from Ipanema*

Call and response .... A style of singing in which the melody sung by one singer is echoed or "answered" by another. Examples include: *My Generation*

Calypso .... A popular song form from the Caribbean island of Trinidad, generally upbeat. Popularized by Harry Belafonte, calypso has an emphasis on acoustic guitars and a variety of percussion instruments, particularly claves, shaker, and bongos. Examples include: *Banana Boat Song*

Cha cha .... An exciting syncopated Latin dance, with a characteristic "cha cha cha" rhythm at the end. Examples include: *Never on a Sunday*

Country Swing . A combination of country, cowboy, polka, and folk music, blended with a jazzy "swing", featuring pedal steel guitar. Examples include: *Lovesick Blues* (Hank Williams)

Disco .... An up-tempo style of dance music that originated in the early 1970s, derived from funk and soul music. Examples include: *Workout, Staying Alive*

8-beat rock .... A staple rock 'n' roll rhythmic pattern with 8 eighth notes in every bar featuring strong accents on beats 2 and 4. The accents are usually emphasized by the drums.

Funk (funky)... A musical style associated with James Brown. The bass features 16th note pickups to the beat, with flourishes of 16th note syncopations in the bass and horns against a rock backbeat. Examples include: *Get on Up*

Gospel .... An African-American religious style featuring a solo singer with heavily ornamented, simple melodies and a dramatic, wide vocal range. The soloist is often accompanied by a choir providing a rich harmonic backdrop. Examples include: *Nobody Knows the Trouble I've Seen*

Jazz .... Jazz encompasses New Orleans Dixieland from the early 1900's, New York stride piano of the 1930's, big-band music from the 1940's, Chicago blues of the 1950's, and atonal free-form music of the 1960's. Jazz has its origins in uniquely American musical traditions, is generally based on chord structures of popular songs from the 1920's to the present, and always features some improvisation.

Jazz ballad .... A song-like jazz style, often for solo piano, with rich chords and an emphasis on beauty of tone. Jazz ballads can be played either as solos or with bass and drums providing support. Examples include: *Jazz Hymn, My Foolish Heart*

Jazz waltz ..... A generally relaxed swing style in 3/4 time. Examples include: *Picnic, Moon River*

Motown .... A style of soul music which originated in Detroit, whose features include the use of tambourine along with drums and a "call and response" singing style derived from gospel music. Examples include: *Motor City, ABC*

Pop ballad ..... A form of slow love song prevalent in nearly all genres of popular music. There are various types of pop ballad, from sixteenth-note ballads, to eight-beat ballads, to swing ballads. There is generally an emphasis on romance in the lyrics. Examples include: *A Matter of Regret, Kiss from a Rose*

Reggae .... A music style from Jamaica, with elements of calypso, rhythm and blues, and characterized by a strong offbeat. Examples include: *Jamaican Market, No Woman No Cry*

Rhythm and blues ...... A style of music that combines blues and jazz, characterized by a strong off-beat and variations on syncopated instrumental phrases.

Shuffle .... Based on the tap dancing style where the dancer, wearing soft-soled shoes, "shuffles" their feet in a swung 8ths rhythm. Examples include: *Train Stop, Lido Shuffle*

16-beat ballad   A song-based style with gentle momentum created by continuous 16th notes in the rhythm, usually provided by the hi-hat cymbal. Examples include: *Killing Me Softly*

Soul .... An African-American style combining elements of gospel music and rhythm and blues.

Stomp .... A lively, rhythmic jazz style marked by a heavy beat. The style derives its name from the stamping of the pianist's heel along with the beat. Examples include: *Grizzly, Black Bottom Stomp* (Jelly Roll Morton)

Swing .... A fun, dance-like style, usually using swung 8ths.

Swung 8ths .... 8th notes that are written normally, but played in this gentle dotted rhythm:

Tango .... A rhythmically strict style, with no off-beat and a snare roll on beat 4. Examples include: *It Takes Two, Hernando's Hideaway*

Thriller feel.... Named after the title song on Michael Jackson's Thriller album, this style has a distinctive bass line and rhythmic feel. The funky bass plays against an 8-beat rock rhythm in a minor key. Examples include: *Bad*

Walking bass .. A bass style which has a note on every quarter note beat of the bar, usually "walking" from one beat to the next in scale tones (either whole or half steps) or along arpeggiated chords. Examples include: *Taking Things in Stride*

Waltz .... A dance in 3/4 time, usually played with a strong accent on the first beat, with weaker beats on beats 2 and 3 in the accompaniment. Examples include: *Edelweiss*